# INTRODUCTION

This generation of the world's inhabitants has a rendezvous with destiny (to paraphrase Franklin Roosevelt in 1936). This census of peoples is called upon as if it represents the chosen ones—chosen to save those who follow us from a disabled and broken down natural world. This is a call we cannot reject because the stakes are too high, the risk is too great.

We are the ones that must face up to the revealing facts emerging daily about this unique Earth. Our greatest gift is diminishing in viability. Its very existence is now at risk because of our negative impact on the air, the water, and the soil.

Things need to be said, things need to be done. Silence and inaction are no longer an option.

Please study this missive. Let us join together worldwide to turn around discordant elements by entering into a new concerted, universal effort to save this delicate, beautiful, unique rock called Earth.

We owe it to our children and grandchildren to stop our culpable behavior, which is likely to turn our habitat into an ignoble funeral pyre, sooner rather than later. Reason and a focused objective must now rule.

Who among us does not care if this magnificent planet turns into a cinder or returns to the very star dust from which it originated 4.5 billion years ago? All must join this plea for a rescue and not a single straggler should be left comfortable in their indifference.

# DEDICATION

This book is dedicated to those political leaders who, because of circumstances beyond their control, now must face Earth's largest challenge.

The top twelve leaders of the world (representing over seventy percent of us) have it within their power at this very moment to lend the seven billion souls of the Earth a new vision—a vision that can lead us all toward the successful rescue of our tormented natural world. We must begin this journey now, and all small voices must become louder. We must support those leaders with the courage to try and lead us all away from a natural disaster emerging in our midst.

# PROLOGUE

The reader may be well served if you know about the author. I have no credentials, no portfolio. I have been an Independent Insurance Agent for over thirty years. But I do know from years of study that our earthly environment is undergoing an unsustainable amount of stress authored by its human inhabitants. The problem grows exponentially. Heat records are broken regularly throughout the world. Climate change is being revealed more than ever and can hardly be disputed.

Like so many others, I want to leave my grandchildren a better world. But without serious immediate action, that hope is becoming quite dim, environmentally.

As the poet Longfellow has suggested: "The laws of Nature are just but terrible. There is no weak mercy in them." (More on Longfellow later.)

The consequences of our abuse are about to become clearer as the climate changes and ice disappears throughout the world. We can expect to suffer for the inequities we have committed against nature. Without our recognizing our wrongs and if we don't amend our behavior, future generations have little chance of survival in the natural world.

Those still in denial, indifferent and in some cases hostile to nature we cannot accommodate, but simply hope they come along eventually on our important journey to survival.

This rescue mission must begin immediately. There is no religious or political test and ethnicity has no bearing whatsoever as we muster the courage and drive to ensure the future of our natural world.

I love sports. I play racquetball twice a week for over thirty years now. I am addicted to baseball and the Detroit Tigers. I follow the saga of Tiger Woods in golf. I am in a bi-monthly poker club. I follow politics. I am opinionated. I have given speeches for one of my principal clients over how to sell insurance. Now I realize none of these things will rescue our earthly garden that is suffering from so much abuse. I must change focus; we all must change. Our priority henceforth must be saving this mysterious rock in space. Now is the time, this is the place.

My explanation for a lack of bibliography? I have seen authors list fifty pages, yet their research and outcomes often remained specious, in my judgment. I have read, observed, and now believe that postponing remedial steps towards our habitat will lead to negative consequences. Anyone who reads newspapers or watches television can observe an environment that is stressed.

As far as my poetry, I simply tried to embrace truth. I harbor no illusions that the critics will give any of them an A+. I embrace poetry as a form of expression.

Thank you for reading my strategy for what should be and can be an exciting ride to the rescue for an Earth undergoing a great deal of pain.

# TRIFLING WITH NATURE

Hell is truth seen too late
Duty neglected in its season
Tryon Edwards

A reminder: I have no portfolio, I have few science creden-
tials. But I can clearly see truth being hidden in the cellar, truth
hidden in the attic, environmental truths denied and ridiculed.
Witnessing this has caused me to take action.

Our environmental world is burning, melting, drowning, and
changing dramatically. Too many authors of this mess remain in
denial. Some act as if proven facts are inconsequential, while they
strike a pose of indifference. We simply cannot wait for the conver-
sion of those proud of their blindness over environmental issues. If
they care not for the Earth's future as well as the future for their own
children as they embrace ridicule toward those who do care, then
how is it those very people get to thwart a rescue mission? Using
arguments that this globe has heated up before from causes such as
asteroids, a tilted Earth, sun spots, or what have you, is meaningless.
Ice core samples going back 400,000 years show a dramatic increase
in $CO_2$ in just the past hundred years. Man is responsible for these
extraordinary emissions. This Earth is undergoing a change and it
is dramatic. It can indeed be argued that hell may be just around
the corner if we choose not to mend our environment.

The way out of our environmental mess—the way to rescue this man-created junk yard of our atmosphere, our water, and our soil—is to enact honor, respect, and partnering with nature. Tokenism makes some feel good, but our destiny requires vastly more purpose by vastly more people than we now witness.

Our natural world is bending toward chaos ever so surely, hour by hour, moment by moment. The question is, when will it be irreparably broken? Gambling that nature will wait several decades for us to heal the wounds of disrespect is, in my opinion, the biggest gamble that mankind will ever mistakenly embrace. Now is the time to begin the reparations. We owe it to nature; we owe it to our children. A competent recognition of our situation should be our best beginning over how to move forward.

# THE PROBLEM

The author wants to state that saving this Earth is not a Christian problem, a Muslim problem, a Jewish problem, a Hindu problem, nor is it the problem of any other major religion or the problem of the atheist. Climate change has been authored by all of us and it must be solved by all of us.

Those founders of the U.S. Constitution did not create a religious document. In fact, they suggested there would be no religious test to hold office in the United States.

Similarly in World War II, the Allies did not suggest that only the religious need fight the war. Everyone was drafted. The United States went so far as to accommodate over 25,000 conscientious objectors, allowing them to avoid combat, through alternative service.

Our war to accommodate and repair nature will require an all-out effort of all religions, all peoples rich and poor, all nations rich and poor, as we recapture the high ground for the natural world.

Excuses over why we will fail, why we cannot afford it, etc., are meaningless. Who in their right mind would discount a safety net for their children's future?

I was a draftee in the Army in 1957, stationed at a small quartermaster depot, south of Paris, France. We were billeted in tarpaper shacks. Two months after I arrived, there was a fire in the middle of the night. I was awakened by a friend, yelling about the fire and to run. I asked him where the fire was and he yelled: "Three shacks down from ours." I remember rolling over and instructing him to call me when the shack next to ours was on fire. This anecdote describes most of us in the world over climate change. We will get a sense of urgency when the water is lapping near the lobby of Miami's rich hotels on the Atlantic Ocean. By then, of course, remedial action will be way too late.

My prayer is we all can learn a lot if we see the problem clearer and prepare now for action.

We all have lives filled with programs, pursuits, and professions. Many focus on vocational survival while bringing up their children to avoid drugs and wrong doing. Some, unfortunately, do not even have a job. Social ills often keep us from our major environmental problems that are now looming larger and larger each year. No one can guarantee that nature will wait for us to begin remedial steps in reversing the $CO_2$ that is already past the danger point of 350 parts per million in our atmosphere.

Below are ten simple reasons to mount a worldwide major undertaking by a majority of the seven billion souls on Earth:

1. Why are a vast majority of ice bodies in the world in remission? When ice melts that is on land, it runs often into a major ocean, causing levels to rise. Secondly, it reveals land that absorbs the sun's rays. So the sun formerly reflecting off the ice, now adds to our heat problems as ground is uncovered. Ice that melts while resting on a body of water, the North Pole for example, does not affect water levels in the ocean. However, dissipated ice reveals surface water

that also absorbs sunlight and adds more heat to the equation. Most major glacial and Greenland ice are in retreat, and in retreat exponentially in many cases, while surpassing predictions. Glacier National Park has lost 75% of its glacial ice since 1850. Again, landlocked ice leaves open earth that absorbs sunlight after a meltdown. But in some worse cases, glaciers turned to ice melt give up their annual fresh water source to local inhabitants, like Peru and Nepal for example. Losing ice worldwide is not just leading to oceans rising, but when glaciers recede, the impact is local as well, as fresh water supplies are endangered.

2. Forest removal also has a detrimental effect, especially rain forests that cool the air and absorb $CO_2$, giving up oxygen in the process. As forest disappears the actions of the sun are provoked because of the displacement. Now heat-absorbing land is revealed or in just as many cases, asphalt, cement, and buildings replacing the trees absorb huge amounts of sunlight. We would do well to remember, millions of buildings and a million miles of heat absorbing roads of concrete and asphalt add to the heat equation of the Earth. None of these losses to heat are in remission. Displacement continues ever so surely as mankind continues to expand to accommodate seven billion souls.

3. Most major rivers of the world are used as one form of sewer deposits or another. From the air, you can observe the deltas of these major rivers turn the ocean to a muddy, dirty grey/brown. The run off deposits are so toxic in many cases that we now call

those areas a "dead zone" because of the lack of oxygen that is pushed out by farm fertilizers, human sewage, and industrial waste. For every step we take forward, growth and convenience forestalls lasting remedies to most of the Earth's major rivers. The damage done to our oceans in the form of acidity is now provable and increasingly so.

4.  The permafrost in Alaska, Canada, and Siberia is now threatened by rising temperatures. The meltdown is going lower and lower into the ground and becoming more dangerous as time passes. Methane is released as these areas warm. Methane is more potent and has more of an immediate effect in the atmosphere than $CO_2$. The Arctic areas of the world are experiencing warmer and warmer winters, sometimes twenty degrees above normal. This does not bode well for permafrost areas that have been in this condition for over a decade. The results are the "drunken forest" effect as trees lean over, roads collapse, and buildings become unstable. Is the condition reversible? In our new world of rescue and confronting the problem, we had better find out, because we cannot wait until 2050 to face up to this threat. A methane release of this possible magnitude is bound to have consequences.

5.  Our oceans are feeling the effect of being used as a giant toilet bowl by man. The acidity of the oceans is rising as fouled air effects the surface and as waste is dumped into them. Phytoplankton algae in the oceans that capture carbon dioxide and give off oxygen are in steep decline. The ability of the oceans to handle our waste is finite. We have ocean gyres that

spin billions of tons of waste in an unending nightmare. In the North Pacific Ocean there is a gyre twice the size of Texas that captures the flotsam and rides it in a giant swirl, so disgraceful that only the most brazen of our race would not become upset over this ocean junkyard we have created.

6. Our coral reefs are dying of heat, disease, and pollution. Just as the rain forests provide much of our medicine, we also discover medicinal reasons to appreciate the coral reefs of the world. They hold exotic fish and exotic beauty, and act as a measure of the ocean's health. The evidence is mounting that these reefs are losing the battle of vitality and their shrinkage cannot be argued.

7. Our heated atmosphere is rising a foot or more a year up mountain ranges. This means foliage increases skyward. This means insects can thrive where they were not known to thrive in the past. This means higher elevated snow cover and glaciers are more and more at risk. Can we reverse the trend of negative human activity? The usual answer: can we afford to remain static as if actions are useless?

8. We are losing unique plants and animal species daily, especially from our rain forests. Some of these plants give us medicine. We still have not identified all fishes, animals, or insects in the world. Instead many will be gone and any derivative for mankind leaves with them.

9. Our inland fresh water, our water tables, rivers, and lakes, need us to care. As needs for seven billion of

us grows, through habitat, drinking water, and food sources, all systems will be strained without proper planning and thoughtful design for the future. The days of let's hope everything will turn out okay without a full scale, hands on approach are over. We are close to our last out at the plate and headed possibly toward a dugout of hell.

10. More unknown ramifications of our environmental negligence will probably arise in less than a decade. Our use of 30% of our corn crops for bio-fuel can threaten food supplies if we have crop failures. Russia lost 20% of its crops in 2010 due to unusual hot weather. We can only pray that these unforeseen negatives that may arise are manageable. The best way to prepare for future shocks is to embrace our fiduciary duties immediately. As we embrace good stewardship, we can only hope our awareness is timely, and that our newfound affection for the natural world does not go unrequited, by Mother Nature.

Factually, how much more evidence do we need that our first priority is saving the natural world? We must never forget that most predictions over how badly the natural world is doing falls short of reality. Our world is on an exponential path of heating up and melting down at an alarming rate.

Keep reading to get an explanation over how we can roll on to victory.

# MIND EXPANSION

The laws of Nature are just, but terrible. There is no weak mercy in them. Cause and consequence are inseparable and inevitable. The elements have no forbearance. The fire burns, the water drowns, the air consumes, the Earth buries...

Longfellow

Longfellow thought abuses of nature would lead to inevitable consequences as nature is "unerring in her judgments." We must admit to the diminishing health of the natural world. We must recognize the need to begin restoration by nurturing and addressing those abuses that have put us all in jeopardy. The correct way to protect our children's' future is to perform our obligations to nature right now.

We need limitless imagination as we tackle the necessary world of curing our environmental ills. The science we need, to correct decades of wrongdoing toward our natural world, is available right now. It is simply suffering from disuse atrophy. We have not challenged ourselves to stop the pollution of our atmosphere, our water, and our soil. Urgency and necessity will make us focus—make us see possibilities heretofore hidden because of indifference. Imagination can rule our actions—cause inventive behavior, and exciting new ways to put mankind on a positive track. Rescuing nature is a noble venture, a positive action. Pity those who cannot see the need to change and grow in a reborn and remade world.

Our efforts to date, through recycling, better use of scrap metal, paper, cans, concrete, rubber, etc., sadly only amount to tokenism. More population, more automobiles, more coal power plants, more roads, more buildings, offset former good intentions. The problem solving must be of the WWII type—all out for survival. Remember the United States went from military training with wooden rifles in 1941 to an atomic bomb four years later. We went from four aircraft carriers to 59 in five years. We made liberty ships in thirty days. We produced more steel than our opponents Japan and Germany combined. The Western Allies in WWII were mostly of one mind. Cooperation among different cultures was remarkable. That spirit of a united world and literally a united nations is now what we are called upon to acquire again. Failure to rally as a human race is too consequential to dwell on. Our natural world can be our friend and partner if we act now, accommodate now, and move to repair our negligent behavior now. The healing of nature, the resurrection of nature, must be our central theme, our cultural *raison d'etre!*

# ARTICLES OF CONFEDERATION

Less government, lower taxes, more state rights? That has already been tried in this country, and it led to a resounding failure, authored by the Articles of Confederation. Shortly after we defeated the British, that document was created as: "The Firm League of Friendship." It was a fiasco from the start. It simply hatched tumultuous disunity on a new nation, because of its loose and non-binding arrangement over power. There was no power to tax, print money, maintain a military, or regulate commerce between the states. The thirteen colonies had simply struck a non-binding clamorous unequal arrangement. After the several years of floundering, George Washington finally commented that: "We are fast verging to anarchy and confusion."

The result was fifty-five representatives of the Colonies met in 1787 in Philadelphia to form a more "perfect union." Our present Constitution was simply created as a means to lend order and decency among the governed of our young nation. The Articles of Confederation contained few political adhesives to bind us together. Our present form of government under Federalism provides that glue to keep us viable. Over 220 years later, that glue still holds a majority of our citizenry to a common thread. We need the voter to know that a loose federation does not work. The Civil War, at a cost of 600,000 lives, confirmed a union of states led by a central power. Throughout our history, that central power concept has been honored. We all should want it honored for 200 more years.

We have to pay taxes, honor our government, and lend our leaders our best thoughts and prayers. Anarchy should and cannot be revisited in the name of disdain for our own government and its institutions. Especially when so many of the complaints are groundless on their face. Our duly elected representatives are in Washington to pass laws and to promote the general welfare and all the rest. They were not sent there to block progress and babysit old documents and old buildings, while collecting handsome benefits.

Every eighth grader in America was taught the above insights through their civics or social studies, the same way I was as an eighth grader by Helen Miller. Why do so many now disregard these truths and try to cash in by fomenting disdain and hostility toward their own government and the duly elected opposition? The enemy is not those willing to pay taxes and honor their government. The enemy might be those who sow hatred and distrust over the proper authority of the Constitution. We all must gather around the same flag, the same Constitution, and use our energies in advancing a just society for all of our citizens. Otherwise we face condemnation by the forces of history and God, in my judgment.

Let us repair to the task at hand, in the spirit of those in Philadelphia over 200 years ago.

# THE U.S. CONSTITUTION AND THE WORLD

Arguably the greatest assemblage of men with good intentions occurred in 1787 when fifty-five delegates gathered in Philadelphia to repair the Confederation Congress. The new American country was governmentally ineffective under the Articles of Confederation. George Washington said (as I stated earlier), it is "fast verging to anarchy and confusion."

The thirteen separate sovereign states were disunited, with no national purpose, no national defense, no national currency, and no uniform tariffs. There was a need to focus on a stronger, less loose set of principles with which to govern.

Salvation came about with the idea of a strong central government with enough clout to enforce a national will superior to states' rights, while preserving most states' rights. Over a four month period these fifty-five men constructed a document that no doubt will historically rival any other for effectiveness. The U.S. Constitution emerged as a "bundle of compromises." The fact that it has lasted over 220 years, through a civil war, world wars, skirmishes, recessions, depressions, impeachments, and general abuses too numerous to name is a testament to the far sightedness, fair mindedness and brilliance of those authors so many years ago.

Now it seems that document is stressed as the sacrifices of those good men seem forgotten. They chanced getting their necks in a noose had they lost the war against England. After that Revolutionary War and the failure of the Articles of Confederation, they finally did succeed in forming a more "perfect union," to which we should all be grateful. But are we?

The population of the U.S. is a hundred times greater now than in 1787 but it seems we have a hundred times less wisdom. Peace is a dirty word and civility and moderation are interpreted as weakness. Compromise is often rejected. Confronting false premises with truth is not acceptable. Instead it's equivocal stretching of truth. Pundits rule the airwaves with mindless twisting and turning of facts. Rant and hate radio and television fling doctrine and ideology in place of reason at an all too willing audience, who seemingly thrive on and endorse deception. These same radio and television hosts turn good will of religious faith and past tolerances on their ear by mocking the poor, mocking opposition, mocking taxes, mocking government, and disregarding any need to protect the environment. Often these gurus of the airwaves filter their audience phone calls to avoid opposition. Meanwhile they never appear in an open forum where their positions can be tested and debated. Ironically their reluctance to debate is rewarded with a strong listener base. We now seem to have at least 30% of the population ready to accept one party totalitarian rule and to let the U.S. Constitution fade away as "just a piece of paper." We do not reject this segment of our society nor their First Amendment rights, but can only hope they will see the problems of the natural world.

Now is the time for wisdom and vision. We cannot afford a dogmatic totalitarian mindset. What can turn around these mindless political games that seem to engulf us all? A national purpose can get us all pulling together for survival. Look at the environment!

Climate change rules. In the western U.S., wild fires from dryness are on the rise. Beetles are destroying millions of trees as they thrive in a warmer climate. Rainfall is more severe in its intensity. Snow patterns in the 2010/2011 winter season rivaled anything in the past in some areas. Meanwhile the Arctic and Greenland areas are experiencing temperatures as high as twenty degrees above normal in the winter. Much of the world is undergoing dramatic climate change.

The world can no longer trifle with nature. Nature's timetable is becoming much shorter than predicted. A universal position to ensure the future of those generations to follow us is needed. This necessity can cause us to unite in a spirited attack on our environmental ills. Such a resolve will lead to inventiveness on how to proceed and how to succeed.

Herein lies the model of those fifty-five men in Philadelphia in 1787. They won the war against the English. The threat of a noose was gone—but how to govern and bind a nation together? Now our natural world is threatening to put a noose around our necks and that of our children. How to proceed? Past environmental affiliations and attempts at a focused world opinion have failed. We need a two-hundred-country political position carved out at the United Nations level. Each country must send delegates with the power to act on positions and environmental standards that will reverse our meltdown and the accelerating climate change. This gathering must take place to immediately effectuate change. If not, in the alternative, we simply remain adrift and allow unwanted rising waters to lap at Miami, New York, London, and Sao Paulo, as both polar regions and Greenland continue to lose ice cover and pour trillions of tons of fresh water into the oceans.

That spirit of Philadelphia can transfigure the world. Coupled with that spirit can be the World War II model of cooperation by the Western Allies. Those Allies planned and structured victory in a short five-year period. They had not asked for war but when survival was an issue, they responded with mass cooperation and three shifts a day. Unlike WWII, there will be no casualties in this struggle to save our habitat. A world purpose can and should be our salvation. Who in their right mind does not want to take on the responsibility of preserving this amazing third rock from the sun?

In the 1940s as the Western Allies overcame all technical shortfalls to defeat totalitarian enemies, they did so with full United States corporate support. The profit motive remained in place and a war board led by Harry Truman performed admirably by eliminating fraud in the manufacturing community. The government played a large role in the struggle to survive, but it was with the consent of the governed.

That World War II model can be used on a worldwide scale. The motivation and pressure to succeed is hardly different from those threats experienced by the WWII Western Allies. The natural world is threatening us as a form of reprisal for our abuse and indifference and failure to partner with nature. Recognition of these facts and a concerted drive by all to seek amelioration will assuage the problem by a demonstration that nature exists with us and for us. The environment owes us nothing—it is we the people that owe the natural world everything. If we fail to acknowledge a natural hell emerging before our very eyes, then we have jeopardized the well-being of those to follow us.

It would be foolish to believe that evil, ignorance, wizardry, and dumb down politics can be allowed to replace the time to reason and progress, to an improved world.

We would do well to note those cogent words from the Book of Common Prayer, which states:

> We have left undone those things which we ought to
> have done;
> and we have done those things which we ought not
> to have done;
> and there is no health in us.

We must reestablish the health of our natural world. This is the generation, now is the time.

# WALL STREET

Socio-politically Americans are in the vice-like grip of dogma and ideology concerning capitalism and the profit motive. In effect, it has become a dollar-worship concept. Nothing is done in the marketplace without profit. Conceptually this approach sows distrust of government and especially government bureaucracies, taxation, and most things non-business. Too much disrespect of government rules some circles.

Historically when dogma or ideologies trumps reason or spirituality, it shortens the life of the very entity so constrained. Behavior by some pointing to the dollar and profit worship is so ignorant only the blind MBAs on Wall Street continue to promote such totalitarianism. Capitalism and profit have to be earned by good service, good products, and the maintenance of the company's core values. Nowadays, a company can lose money and the CEO still demands a raise to keep pace with his peers. It is such a travesty that it makes the lower classes laugh at the cynicism.

Another false God bites the dust: Ayn Rand, as Wall Street fails and has to run to the U.S. taxpayers for a bailout. Ayn Rand was the proud totalitarian cynical worshipper of the dollar. In fact, she often displayed a piece of jewelry shaped as a dollar sign on her blouse. She remains one of the philosophical heroes for many Wall Street gurus, even though she rejected altruism and charity as a virtue to be pursued. Meanwhile, Bill Gates and Warren Buffet, the two richest men in America, are giving most of their money to charitable foundations while they suggest they are not taxed enough. Henceforth, Ayn Rand followers may want to turn to our Founding Fathers or even a known god for metaphysical support. I seriously doubt that her need to make the dollar an idol to be worshipped was either heaven sent or heaven inspired.

In our country, if a twenty-five-year-old unemployed male with two children robs a bank for $1,000, gets caught, and is convicted, he goes to jail for twenty years. We then pay over $30,000 a year for his upkeep. But a Wall Street investment firm that manipulates the system for a ten billion dollar loss to subscribers is a different story. Not only does no one stand trial (so far), but that firm can be resurrected by going to the government (i.e., "We the taxpayer") for new start-up loans and go right back to business as usual. Then the customers line up quickly to again put their investment portfolio on the line. The investment firm receives very little increase in regulation or oversight. In fact, Wall Street, after new money is borrowed, then again complains about "government interference." Meanwhile, many business pundits on television echo that same cry over how the government is such a bother and a pain for Wall Street to have to tolerate!

When the average taxpayer is told these above examples, the vast majority have little objection to the disparity in penalties and jaded results over criminal interpretations. Furthermore, those of us who see some ironic conclusions to these examples or feel any pain for the bank robber have to then suffer the tag: "Oh, he is soft on crime."

Wall Street is now the largest casino in the world. Even when or if the structure goes awry, with derivatives, swaps, and sub-prime morass, as the investor takes large hits to his investment and pension portfolio, nothing really changes. Then we have to listen to the major players on Wall Street suggest that our Founding Fathers set up "a capitalistic society," one that, by the way, should be venerated and worshiped as closely as any major religion. In fact, when our U.S. Constitution was written, America was a land of farmers and small merchants. Corporate America was still almost a century away from the significant power it now enjoys. That power should never be one similar to an absolute right. It should always and forever be a privilege and not a right to do business in our country. The government of the people, by the people, and for the people is still superior to the largest corporations in America. Otherwise, we may all become relegated to workers for the plantation owners; those owners who can simply afford to buy out all those who may threaten their corporate power. The U.S. Supreme Court has recently blessed that very position, and we allow case law of unlimited corporate political donations to stand at our own peril. Most politicians receiving these donations respond accordingly to the wishes of the donor.

In 2010, Wall Street (after the government bailout) gave out bonuses totaling $20.8 billion. That is fifty times more than the new Treasury Department's Consumer Financial Protection Bureau's recommended budget cap. This information came out in testimony before the House Financial Services Committee.

I have invested in Wall Street; I believe in the profit system but only if it is regulated with oversight. The government correctly runs the country, not corporations. Corporations serve at the pleasure of the people, which has been the case since 1787 and must be so today.

In 1960 the U.S. federal income tax pie reflected that 31% of our tax revenue came from corporations. Today that figure is less than 7%. Ironically, in 1960 the corporate outcry against "government interference" was minor compared to what it is today. The threat of the dominance of corporations in our daily lives in

America is real and present. We have to be on guard against 30,000 lobbyists dominating the masses, which could have the capacity to take us all down in the power struggle. We get what we deserve if we tolerate an economy dominated only by those hands holding the most money. The Constitution of the United States of America was constructed to protect the people and not to offer free license and power to the largest financial corporations. We must strive to make intellect and reason the focus of Congress, not money. For those cynics who laugh at such a principle, the people can have the last say if they will simply exercise their rights.

Wall Street joined the war cause in World War II, and they will be obliged to join in the struggles to put the Humpty Dumpty natural world back together, as part of the reparation team.

Wall Street, no matter how much money they attain, will not be able to stop the expected rising waters around Manhattan Island. It is in their self-interest to accept facts about climate change and to join the march to resolutions and repairing the natural world.

# HOPE

We do not honor and respect nature. We pay little attention to our environment. There are thirty different oak trees in the United States. The average person doesn't care about trees, birds, fishes, or naming the most visible stars out of the 6,000 visible in the night sky. The ancient Greeks studied stars and named them. The American Indian left little evidence or imprints of where they had previously camped. Now, after decades of indifference, we will be forced to love nature and nurture her back to health like a sick child. If we do not, we will suffer the consequences. We now will be forced to give back for our years of neglect.

But, can we still save our habitat? This blue, green, white, brown, and smoggy habitat will still respond to genuine concerted remedial efforts, in my opinion.

Reduction of $CO_2$ is the key. I do not side with those who think we have already jumped off the cliff and now cannot save ourselves, even if we are just halfway down from an inevitable crash. Recognizing the problem, admitting the cause, and resolving to join hands with all seven billion of us will cause hope to replace denial, indifference, and inaction.

The journey will be purposeful, full of a reason to get up in the morning for every one of us. A united single minded adventurous rescue can impress nature and rescue our environment.

Some say it will bankrupt our economy. Some say the challenge is too large. Some have no opinion. Some choose petulance and denial, despite overwhelming and continually growing facts that suggest we are the author of this environmental precarious situation.

To those so situated, we simply move on to a better world and allow them to catch up later. The rational, the reasonable among us, must wrest power and put our broken environment back to a natural, un-tortured state.

# CALL TO ACTION

This is the generation that is left with the trash of all past generations. Upon us has been dumped industrial waste, sulfur dioxide from smoke stacks, dirty water, residual hot air, diminished forests, more insects, acidic oceans and less natural mutualism of atmospheric gasses.

The natural world is responding through the shrinkage of most of the world's major ice bodies. Greenland is three times the size of Texas and is covered with ice a mile and a half deep. That ice is melting into the North Atlantic Ocean at an alarming rate, beyond most prognostications.

Meanwhile in the United States, by October first 2011 the National Weather Service  had already reported a record breaking 83 natural disasters for the year. Kansas City had 20 straight days of temperatures above 100 degrees in July. Texas has had a drought and forest fires damaging an estimated quarter billion dollars worth of property.

For those who still do not believe that these dramatic changing weather patterns should be a cause for alarm, we can only marvel at their blindness. Remaining adrift and in denial in an ocean of change is simply dumb down behavior.

We had better adjust. We need all hands on deck to assuage nature and to reduce stress to the environment upon which we depend for so much life. We need all segments of society to rally around an international purpose geared toward saving the natural world.

We will be fighting for the survival of that natural world. For those who want to wait for the science to become clearer or believe nature will wait a few more decades before serious action is needed – I say no. This is our only earth to gamble with in the show down over ice melt, acidic air and acidic oceans. We cannot wait any longer to practice good stewardship. We have a fiduciary duty to act now and to deny those who want to roll the dice when the future of our children is at stake.

We have it in our power to nullify predictions of end times if we begin immediate steps to partner with the natural world.

Every adult citizen of the world must now demand an answer from their leaders to the following question:

"What are you doing to protect our children's environmental future?"

The answer to that question is our beginning point for the rest of our time on this earth. Who wants to be part of a generation that rejected a chance to come to the rescue?

Our earth is now giving every one of us a chance to have an altruistic reason to get up in the morning. And to get up with a purpose that embraces honorable pursuits.

For centuries humanity has studied astronomy intent upon finding life as we know it in outer space. So far, in the vast arena of the universe we have yet to prove that there exists a comparable rock anywhere. The trillions of celestial bodies have yet to support a notion that life exists there similar to ours. We still appear to be the unique gem in all of space. This being the case lends all the more reason to offer protection to this third rock from the sun. End times may be just around the corner if we reject that thesis.

No, dear reader, let us get up and get moving toward the rescue. We must not go quietly toward the very gates of hell while we can still scratch and fight for the future of our children.

That future will be radically different because of the circumstances we find ourselves entering. Trophies, medals, financial triumphs, and wars will be tossed on a scrap heap of irrelevance henceforth. The new focus will be making sure nature remains alive and well for all of us.

There is no environmental problem that science cannot correct. We have the knowledge at this very moment to save the natural world. We must begin to apply this knowledge through world wide joint ventures. Now we are forced to put a value on time. Failure to act precipitously can turn time into an impatient tyrant. The threat of nature turning against us should clarify and focus our thinking. It should drive us to solutions that offer protection for our children.

If an asteroid ten by twenty miles long was headed toward earth, to strike us in a decade – does anyone believe conscientious citizens would not take preventive measures?

The measures I propose for confronting a natural world meltdown revolve around imitating the origins of the U.S. Constitution and the concerted efforts of the Western Allies in World War II. These two concepts were focused on success as no other in history and similarly for us they may be the key to our survival. Necessarily there must be dramatic changes in our sources of energy, our means of transportation and our willy-nilly growth and expansion patterns. Grand transformational worldwide plans will be the rule, not the exception. If we take a hard look at the consequences of doing nothing then transformation is much better than hell on earth.

Planning, research, and development committees must arise to pick viable alternative energies. We also must find scrubbers to reduce $CO_2$ below 350 ppm in the atmosphere. Necessity and imagination will cause us to find answers for victory just as the Western Allies did in WWII. A concerted effort, a focused goal-driven body of people can make us avoid the revenge of a tormented natural world.

I will never believe that the human race, given all the evidence about global warming and climate change, will reject taking remedial steps toward saving their world. Told their children's lives and future are in jeopardy, who in their right mind would not come to the rescue? That's where we stand at this very moment in history. Act now or leave your children at a polluted sacrificial altar. Why must we leave them dirty air, acidic and depleted water, and exhausted soil? Where is that written?

We must avoid hell. History has chosen this generation. There is precious little time left to make amends.

We have erred by trifling with nature and insulting this marvelous earthly gift. The task of deliverance must begin now while it can still be an exciting and worthwhile journey. The time for good stewardship and exercising our fiduciary duty has arrived.

Let us repair to the moment at hand and move to our individual rescue stations in the spirit of cooperation with each other and with the natural world.

# UNIFYING THOUGHTS

The world is one-third Christian—or at least that is the number of people who profess some form of the Christian faith. One rather startling fact about that faith is there are over 28,000 sects making up the religion. Imagine that faith with a united single purpose. The closest we came to faith lending power and strength was World War II, by the Western Allies.

Since 1945 the Christian faith has waned in influence and participation. There is currently more evidence that the Christian faith is weakening than gaining members. As global warming and climate change becomes a valid concern, it is my contention that all versions of the Christian faith should view the gift of this Earth as something that should be cherished and lent conscientious stewardship. Instead, a unique rock in the universe is tormented and treated in some cases as a convenient junk yard. Honor and respect is absent.

The Muslim faith has stamina and vigor in the religious world, but just as in the Christian faith, the environment and caretaking the Earth is not seen as a great concern.

All faiths large and small must rally around nature in a partnering program henceforth or suffer regrets later.

A world model for attacking and reversing environmental meltdown will be secular, but all religious faiths should seek and ask for guidance from their respective faiths.

Meanwhile, we must not turn capitalism into a theology—one that practices irresponsible behavior that justifies ravaging and burning the Earth without remorse or apology.

Democracies and republics eventually end up in the hands of dictators or tyrants when the people only seek easier and easier answers. There is presently in America a restless, active minority quite willing to forsake our Constitution and to take full control of all aspects of our government. Those who don't like it will be rendered powerless as it has been suggested: at the point of a gun, as the appeal of totalitarian political positions sets in.

Thought control, intolerance, intimidation, double speak, and sophistry, accusing your opponent of doing what you do, all in the name of power is alive and well. "Reason" is a dirty, moderate, progressive, liberal word to be shunned at all costs. Lock-step fakery and blindness is done in the name of ideology—no others need apply. Scream at truth as it is driven to the scaffold with the radical mind carrying yards of rope is an okay proposition. A mean and narrow approach is too often offered, especially by the pundits.

Ironically, tyranny can be strong willed and better organized than the moderate. Historically, the tyrant only needs one-third of the population on his side to gain dictatorial control as the one-third moderate cannot rally well enough, especially as the last third of the population sits idle, afraid, indifferent, or unknowing.

Let us form a majority, full of reasons to join hands in an all-out effort to save our natural world.

———————————

If we permit extremes of wealth for a few and enduring poverty for many, we shall create a social explosiveness and a demand for revolutionary change.
Dwight D. Eisenhower

———————————

When a man dies, the people ask, "What property has he left behind him?" But the angels, as they bend over his grave, inquire, "What good deeds hast thou sent on before Thee?"
Mohammed

———————————

The Mayans' calendar runs out 12-21-2012, which coincides with the "dark rift," our sun aligning with the Milky Way galaxy. This alignment only occurs every 26,000 years. It appears the Mayans were superb star gazers and were able to observe some of these phenomenon in the universal sky. We should all use caution in believing in "the end of the world" predictions, since the end of the world has been predicted by many failed stargazers. They packed their bags at the critical time, yet so far, all of them had to unpack the day after their final day failed to show. In the case of the natural world, it will not be a one day all is lost phenomenon but it appears we are being given plenty of notice a tormented world is evolving.

———————————

God does not choose who gets cancer, who wins the lottery, what city gets hit by a hurricane, or what baseball team wins the pennant. God always rejects the wizardry business and is not preferential or capricious.

Proverb 17:5 suggests: "He who mocks the poor shows contempt for their Maker." Yet there are dozens of pundits in the U.S. on radio and television, making millions of dollars annually, doing that very thing. They are inviting their cheering, listening audience to the very gates of hell in so doing, in my judgment.

---

Jesus Christ gives us all a great lesson in economics if we would only listen. He sought social justice through caring for the weakest most vulnerable in our midst while remaining suspicious and wary of the rich. Today in the U.S., we imprison more than any other society and tilt all economics in favor of the rich and corporations. The best way to accomplish a just society is from the bottom up, not from the top down. Do the economic math: an unjust society will wilt and die as baseness, and the veneration of wealth and corporate power dominates our every move.

---

We are fast becoming a nation without a conscience, especially in the area of incarceration of criminals. We now house more convicts than any nation in the world. Vengeance and long sentences rule. Some states budget more for criminality than for higher education. It is fast bankrupting us as a nation—both morally and financially.

> Sidney Harris, a columnist from Chicago, wrote these prescient words in 1969: "Other people may despair about what they call the 'lower classes.' But I don't. I despair more about the 'upper classes.' About the affluent, the educated, the influential, and the basically ignorant. The magazine *Nation's*

*Business* asked its affluent educated and influential readers this spring: "How can we get law and order?" The overwhelming answer came back: "Get tough with lawbreakers." This is so basically ignorant that even the most ignorant member of the lower classes would laugh at it. It doesn't work, it never has, and it never will. This is the cancer on our body politic. It has nothing to do with "coddling" or the Supreme Court or permissive parents. It has everything to do with public corruption, private hypocrisy, and gross inequities in the law. Until we know this, we ourselves are criminally ignorant."

In my state, a decade ago a "get tough on criminals" governor once stated about prison cell shortages: "Stack them like cord wood!" My state now spends much more on prisons than our universities. This attitude of just locking them up is now so costly, we are stuck in deplorable budget problems. Some 35% of the prison population is in for illegal drug use or sales of marijuana. Rehabilitation, job training, sympathy, or recognizing any human qualities in the prisoner is absent. We are now one of the harshest countries in the world, proven in full by our handling of the criminal element. We have lost our Christian conscience and our voice of the soul over our treatment of criminals. It is bankrupting our government and our souls.

---

The American public harbors some graphic misconceptions regarding foreign aid. The reality is, we are no longer a giving nation. Our so-called foreign aid has gone from over three percent of our federal budget in 1960 to under one percent currently.

---

Our world has nearly 50,000 tree species. In the U.S. we have over 600 species. We need to know that these trees are part of our habitat, that they have value, and that we are all better off if they remain alive and well.

---

As America suffers through a crisis of debt, we are witnessing pressure on the have nots to take less and pay more toward our debt reduction. We want them to take less benefits and wages and in some cases, to tax their pensions. Meanwhile, the rich and corporations are spared the sacrifice of having to pitch in. When we declared war on Iraq while cutting taxes at the same time, it was obvious irresponsible politicians were in control as they dumped so much future debt on their own children and grandchildren.

---

Who said you cannot escape taxes? That now is a clear fact for many, far too many Americans. They thrive during two wars and politicians are content to squeeze the lower 50% of America for more and more. Ironically many wealthy Americans are willing to pay more taxes if asked.

The military industrial complex, Wall Street, and the oil lobby are fully in charge of the destiny of the average American citizen. Change, which is so vitally needed to keep us a relevant nation, may come too late as myopia grips so many.

---

A vigorous national purpose involving environmental issues wherein all citizens partake would drive down crime, unemployment, drug use, citizen malaise, and a host of other maladies confronting this nation.

---

## Wealth

If you acquired wealth in America, you are often held up to great esteem and thought of as intelligent. In the end, money has absolutely no currency in heaven. Anyone who thinks the size of their wallet will have an impact on judgment day will only cause the angels to chuckle at the absurdity.

## Health Insurance

The United States is the only major industrialized nation without a universal healthcare plan. Our indifference to forty-two million Americans without health insurance demonstrates that we do not seek a just society as envisioned by our Founding Fathers. It escapes most Americans that it is more of a burden to our federal budget to fail to pass a healthcare plan. Meanwhile, Medicaid is overwhelmed by the uninsured, who appear in emergency rooms all over the United States. This situation is a burden to every state in the union.

Man is too often defiant and in denial over the poor among us. One only has to read of the rich man and Lazarus in the Bible (Luke 16:19–31) to grasp what is in store for those so positioned. Proverbs, in the Old Testament, defends the poor and has ample warning about the danger of mocking those less fortunate.

---

Reason and spirituality are more powerful than dogma, doctrine, and unbendable notions. One lends life and hope, and the other proudly embraces frozen principles.

---

How is it some say Social Security benefits and Medicare do not fit into a just society? The Social Security Administration is the most well-run bureaucracy in the world. Fifty percent of the beneficiaries have no other source of income to keep them out of poverty. Medicare is the last hope of the elderly—who wants to eliminate it and why?

---

When a society spends more of their budget on prisons than universities, you can make a safe bet that society is in a moral meltdown.

---

When a society begins to malign the teaching profession and educational systems, you can bet our children's future is in jeopardy. Without respect and honor offered to the education system, a moral crisis is at hand.

---

The United States is suffering through a disdain of government, a disdain of education and a disdain of the weak members of society. Meanwhile the rich and corporations are venerated. No society can survive such tribulation, nor should they, according to the laws of nature and religion.

---

The most successful economic philosophy is that one that strives to convert the poor into working citizens. Jobs create a tax base. Jobs create purchasing power. Almost one hundred years ago, Henry Ford gave his workers five dollars a day, knowing they could then afford to purchase his cars. President Bill Clinton, in his eight years in office, had twenty-two million additional jobs added in the marketplace. For those who hold that future historians will overlook that fact, guess again!

Now in America, it is a race to deprive workers of more and more benefits. Fatten up corporations while making the rich richer is the current philosophy. Some still argue that this approach will trickle some crumbs down to the lower classes, so why worry? History has proven over and over again that this formula is a case of propaganda over reason and reality.

The excessively greedy have little regard for the poor and pay little mind to the humanity of our race. The strongest and most powerful in the marketplace "take all approach" is truly a jaded mantra. Federal taxation remains the single best way to introduce the greedy to economic reality, while saving our government coffers in the process. Our system is crumbling in the face of low taxation as we are engaged in three wars, heavy unemployment, and a disdain for anything governmental. The middle class simply cannot shoulder all of the debt as the wealthy pay lower taxes than ever before in modern times, especially while we are at war.

The federal deficit, health care, and jobs are America's pressing problems right now. However, the fourth leg of the stool that has the potential to harm the nation is redistricting or gerrymandering as it were. There is a narrow group that can elect Congressmen that show up in Washington with ideology replacing reason and debate. This approach frustrates truth and good government and allows minority views too often to win the day. Undue tension and totalitarian points of view can unravel this republic if it is left unchecked.

Privatization

Privatization is another buzz word that connotes anti-government, pro-corporation. One of the biggest demonstrations of the melting down of America's social fabric is public sector division being sold off to privatization. A school district wants some ready cash and decides to sell their school busing operation to a corporation. So then how does the corporation intend to make a profit on the deal? "Why we'll cut the wages of the bus drivers, take away their health insurance and their pensions!" This scenario is happening all across America and is an excellent example of how the so-called profit motive can destroy us. No pensions, no health insurance is a step forward in the marketplace for our workers? What a crock sold to the consumer, who more than likely will have to pick up the shortfall on health issues and a lack of pension for these bus drivers. The public will no doubt pay a lot to make up what corporate America profited from these drivers.

We invaded the country of Iraq, a country that posed no threat to us and had no military of any consequence. We violated all precepts and tenets of our own government. We killed hundreds of thousands of innocent Iraqi civilians, including displacing or killing the Chaldean population that Saddam Hussein had protected. The society of Chaldeans that spoke Aramaic, the language of Jesus Christ, has been nearly annihilated. Many of the 500,000 Chaldeans have been murdered, threatened, and exposed to so many other dangers that they have fled the country. Men have sinned by their silence on the issue of Iraq. After WWII, the U.S. tried and convicted mass murderers, violators of the Geneva Convention, and water boarders from WWII. Some day somehow our nation will have to make amends for what we did to the Iraqi population. The ends cannot justify the means.

We injured innocent Iraqis, then we shot ourselves in the foot by declaring war and cutting taxes at the same time, thereby transferring the financial liabilities for the wars in Iraq and Afghanistan to our children. We need to reestablish the moral high ground.

---

We will all be judged more on what we did than what we said.

We in America are engaged in the "big lie." Simply put, we think we can solve our fiscal problems by not taxing the rich or corporations more. In my state, it is the teachers and pensioners who are a target for salary reduction and taxes on pensions, while the well off get cuts in hopes the trickle down effects kicks in.

Meanwhile, we spend more on prisons than on our universities. Yet the prison budget remains sacrosanct. When you consider the fact that we imprison more people per capita than any country in the world, and for a longer period, at that point, we must question our wisdom. Societies fail when moral courage is absent. We pretend we value life, but put criminals in permanent dungeons, stacked three high, four feet apart, and 300 to a room as is done in California. Now you can believe we may have reverted to an era darker than the dark ages.

The cost of such treachery in state budgets, to say nothing of the lack of righteous indignation, demonstrates how far we have fallen as a nation.

There are lobby groups in our country that threaten our tax code and foil attempts to pay for two wars by allowing the wealthiest Americans to remain on the side lines in supporting our military. Instead, our children and grandchildren will be stuck with the bill for the two longest wars in our history. Historians will no doubt label these "the credit card wars."

Meanwhile these "no tax" lobbyists get rich themselves. You can bet they have those ribbons stuck to their cars that say "support our troops."

It is beyond me how the voting public can abide in such treachery. It is beyond the pale that politicians are intimidated by these lobbyists who put the interests of the country last by refusing to give our troops tax support. Historians will not over look the fact that Iraq and Afghanistan wars were declared while cutting taxes on the wealthy.

To quench fear we spend billions and billions in the U.S. Homeland Security, the FBI and dozens of other federal and local agencies have anti-terrorist capabilities. The trouble is in 2010 more people were killed in the U.S. on bicycles than by terrorists. Now we are told the terrorist threat will not go away for decades, justifying more billions spent.

We have now entered a political era where fear has created permanent bureaucracies that cannot justify their existence. In the meantime, we go broke seeking ultimate safety, as domestic criminal law is bankrupting us.

---

A twenty-five-year-old burglar who has invaded three houses at different times over several years accumulating "three strikes" is now in jail for life. The fact that his criminal gain may be below $7,500 in value is discarded. He costs $35,000 a year upkeep with full medical, clothes, and food. We seem engaged in ideology over reason. Here also love of neighbor, respect and love for all people low, high, or criminal, is now an ancient concept that presently has little currency in America. The concept of stack 'em like cordwood and throw away the key gets too many politicians elected to office, so the public seems oblivious to the cost of their fears and hostilities.

My religious perspectives are slanted toward the Christian view but by no means do I discount Atheists, Muslims, Jews, and Eastern religions. The U.S. was founded upon a viewpoint that all faiths are tolerated, and under our U.S. Constitution, no religious tests are required to become a citizen or to hold public office. We simply must never stray from that principle. If I might suggest the Almighty is not uncomfortable with that position in the least, in my judgment. All hands are needed to save this unique third rock from the sun. A willingness to see that a rescue of our great spatial gift is at hand. No religious or political test required. The human race is too often driven to make sacrificial offerings at their chosen religious altars.

The religious gift we must leave at the altar for those who follow us is a resurrected natural world. Nothing will make God or the angels applaud more than to witness us recognizing the need to partner with nature.

And for non-believers, love of kin, love of nature, may be why you want to pass on a viable natural world.

So let us rid ourselves of doctrinaire reasons not to cooperate over the need to salvage our natural world.

Politicians can play musical chairs, they can play let's pretend, they can deny facts to make life temporarily easier, but eventually taxation will have to be addressed as a way out to help with our ongoing wars and all the other budget shortfalls. The rich and the powerful can run and hide only so long before reality takes hold. Many of our wealthiest citizens expect the tax code to tilt against their wallets. Not so surprisingly, several billionaires in the U.S. encourage higher income taxes and higher estates taxes, to save our country from falling into third-world status.

These revenue problems all started when Washington, D.C., never protested starting two wars and cutting taxes at the same time. The military personnel were the only segment of the U.S. population asked for sacrifices. Disgracefully we now are witnessing almost as many military suicides as those killed in combat. Over half the U.S. population wants to stop so many military operations beyond our borders. We disgrace ourselves with our military policies, as we put so many of our military in harm's way without adequate justification or explanation. A disturbed psyche is often the result of our foreign policy.

––––––––––––

Food for fuel when we are now at seven billion people worldwide and experiencing climate change is a questionable concept. Hunger is now a valid concern for the world.

As a Brazilian physician, Josue de Castro stated years ago: "Hunger is the most degrading of adversities; it demonstrates the inability of existing culture to satisfy the most fundamental necessities, and it always implies society's guilt."

We are morally corrupt as a nation if we do not confront the issue of hunger at a cabinet level. All farming henceforth should be food for the masses, not crops for vehicular fuel. A just society demands that very premise.

––––––––––––

Too often the elderly go out the way they came in: falling down, crying, wetting their pants, and having to be spoon fed.

––––––––––––

Always accept truth—or risk hell in the denial thereof.

———————

The Earth is unique and a gift, why deny it?

———————

We can run from our environmental problems, but nature knows it will not be a very short run. Denying nature as a partner in life is a fatal error.

———————

Without a vision, the people perish is a truism for every generation, and materialism is not a vision. (The time for improvement is always now.) There is always plenty of room for improvement.

———————

Never forget, eternity is a very long time, especially if you are feeling hell's heat.

The New Testament implores Christians (per Jesus Christ, St. Peter, and St. Paul), to "pay your taxes, honor your government, and pray for those in authority." Over seventy percent of U.S. citizens profess some form of the Christian faith but many reject the above admonitions out of hand.

Reasonable men are now forced to do passionate good deeds on behalf of the natural world. Our passion must surpass that of the short-sighted and unreasonable evil doers who want to cultivate havoc and disinformation. Reason and thoughtfulness must put forth a counterbalance.

In World War II, many taxpayers voluntarily sent in excessive contributions to the I.R.S. Imagine that! Now it is, don't pay for wars, don't honor your government, arm yourselves against your own duly elected government, demean the poor, throw away the keys over prison inmates, deny the Geneva Convention, defend water boarding and hanging leaders of countries that pose no threat to us. Those Americans who justify and patronize for this behavior may experience a bitter end game, when all is said and done.

---

So nature designed the panda bear, the seahorse, the trapdoor spider, the puffin, and the Arctic tern? Is nature a designer or simply a keeper of the earthly zoo? Perhaps in the final analysis, nature is simply a partner with a Creator. Charles Darwin proved there may be an evolution of the species but as to their origin, there remains plenty of evidence about a designer. That designer had a sense of humor.

---

Another planet with life as we know it in the vast universe? There is absolutely no proof yet of such suspicion, as we remain the only known "living" planet. Many stargazers argue that lack of proof so far is not proof that we are alone amongst the trillions of stars and rocks across the sky.

———————

Do we have proof that God exists? Well no, not really. It is still a matter of faith and hope for some and absolute denial by others. But wisdom might suggest that because so many of our most brilliant citizens believe in God, then maybe we mere mortals should not be laughed at for our faith. Werner von Braun the German rocket scientist was asked why he believed in a God/Creator. He said, "Because there is so much order in the universe." Some say man invented God and many more hold that God invented man. The mystery will only be fully answered after our mortal coil is removed. Perhaps that's the way it should be—fearing a judgment day can only make a better world, is that not true?

Truth is salutary and lies are bacteria.

———————

Some people think if they can simply deny truth long enough it will vanish with their disavowal. However, truth always survives darkness and attempted drowning.

———————

Truth is concrete, half truths are sand, and lies have no substance as they eventually fizzle in the light of day.

------

Truth has no mind. It cannot think, but it can act. If left unattended too long, its weight can crush us all.

------

Truth in the United States has now become just another political opinion. If it goes against the frozen ideology of certain politicians, truth is frequently discarded.

# POETRY PROLOGUE

We need to re-establish poetry as a means of expression and imagination. Poetry is nearly as old as our species.

I make no assertion that the enclosed poetry will meet with critical acclaim. My purpose in poetry is to simply exploit a means of expression too often overlooked.

# POETRY— NATURE

# FIN

End time, sad time, no preamble,
Our earthly stay a million years before Pericles?
Green, clean spots now dirty parched and hot
Permafrost excessive wet with rot
Releases deadly methane easily
Nature weeps but will show no mercy,
Those who care drowned out
The blind, the dumb are in the fight
Their voices shrill from truth in flight.
Those authors of the end quite near
Find nature hardly dear
Duties denied, arrogantly glad?
Shallow of mind, escaping thoughts sad.
Intellect held up to suspicion
A regrettable truth since Creation
Forests and lakes absent of wonder.
The seas rise as ice dissolves and land goes under,
The swift tern and polar bear may not endure
Their journey no longer safe and pure.
Oh, nature, how to address our plight
How can we restore our sight?
Is the answer seen in the wind,
A wind moving swiftly in the end
Finding us wanting and acting adverse
To save the pearl of the universe
Perhaps unable to escape our fate.

Failed fiduciary duty and stewardship
Accepted during our long, long trip.
Can hope now move us to see more
Glimpsing the Mesozoic era of the dinosaur?
May God not find us free of action
No tears, no dreadful doom, only nature's restoration!

# NATURE

Final Chapter

Four and a half billion years ago
The Earth emerged from stardust
Unfolding into a remarkable story
With so much mystery and glory.
Water and climate, symbiotic elements
Uniquely emerging for the coming moments.
An atmosphere so blended and balanced
Giving rise to flora and fauna nuances
Surrounded by predictability and order
Man arrived during rainbows and thunder,
Such reliable physics lends credibility
To an intelligent design possibility.
But now man's dominance reveals a chance
That nature is abused beyond saving
The atmosphere now too warm
And no one will heed the alarm
Good stewardship flounders feebly
As nature marches to imbalance quickly
Our days are cloudy with indifference
To this Earth's former magnificence
Few plans for change heeded
As fiduciary duties needed

Nature and God so casually disregarded
As now our world an object discarded
Denial and death march together
As vengeful clouds gather
Action and hope must be the order.

# NATURE WEEPS

We must rescue the garden

We must save our children

We must craft a future

We must flee hell

We must rebuild heaven

We must love the task

We must never tire

We must restore grace to nature

All may still be well.

# NO PURPOSE

One flag, one country, one people
Confused, conflicted, lacking purpose
Power defused with unintelligible obstructions
And divisive political abstractions
Little sense of history
No sense of a great story
As nature and economics seek allegory
We show no grasp of history
An unclear path of where we are going
Less knowledge of where we have been
Denial of obligation to save our kin
As usual, truth is on the scaffold
As too many offer a rope to hold.

We must stop this lack of reason
And rediscover Washington and Jefferson
Who fought for political order
And demanded sacrifices of every leader
Most of the world absent of vision
When we need a great decision
Ice melting worldwide, oceans acidic
The flora and fauna challenged
As contaminated air, water and soil
Warn us to expend more toil.

# MYSTERY REMAINS

Are we the center of the universe?
Still no proof otherwise.
A trillion stars across the sky
Where did they come from and why?
Galaxies, nebula, and black holes
The final stages of a star
Exciting scientific wonder from afar
Could it all be an illusion
Since light years obscure a conclusion?
The mystery continues unabated
Answers far too long we have waited.
Galileo, Copernicus, and Einstein still not sure
What we can ascertain in the future.
Until then we can only peer skyward
As the heavens may confirm His Word.

# AMERICA, AMERICA

All societies peak and end
Our *fini,* just around the bend?
America now shallow
America now fallow
No purpose, no vision
Materialism, sports, only in season
Rally around the flag, boys
Thwarted by the pursuit of toys
Government discounted and taxation an enemy
No longer champions of liberty
No longer ready to sacrifice.
No courage to toss the dice
For good over evil,
As we fought off the devil.
This last generation with a chance
To invigorate our old stance
Together the world can be subjugated
To a pristine glory of times obligated
Where is the will, where is the victory
So little time to avoid tragedy.

# POETRY—RELIGION

# GOD AS MAN

A new man in town, different.
A prophet, a philosopher, prescient.
His goal, a just society
Not just added piety.
He ate and drank with sinners
Then made them followers
He offered unique commands
Sacrifices and demands
Loving your enemies, unlimited forgiveness,
Taking care of the weak and helpless
He cured the blind, the sick, the frail
And the dead were released from their jail
Assertions (not denied) that He was God
Made the contemporary religion mad
They felt threatened by such power
So acceptance was not an option
Escape was through a contrived crucifixion
He who came to love and to save
Was demeaned, tortured to His grave
The rejection was painful, soulful.
Hung from a tree but divinity successful
The resurrection denied death
The message lives on for eternity.
Truth denied but not sustainably.

# TELL THE POPE

Tell it to the Pope
That we need a new era of hope
A new era of love
We must accept more heed from above
Then bring the 28,000 Christian sects
To a more united text
The power of the Word
Is too defused to be heard
Our faith has become weak
Our faith has become meek
There is no common purpose
No directed goals for success
Questionable sins is all we protest.
We lack the love of our enemies
The love of our neighbor
We must love the unlovable more,
The weak, the hungry and the poor
Who lack their honor and sympathy
The enemy is materialism and apathy
When the real mystery of the faith
Is still revealed by those least in our path
Too many living absent of this vision
And our environment lacks a position
Such little desire for allegory
That would transfigure us to glory
Too many crucifying truth in the land
A universal renewal must be at hand.

# FAILED DIRECTION

No sense of history,
No national purpose,
No one ready to propose.
This perverse generation does not mind
Future generations left behind.
Millions absent of any vision
Unprepared for a great decision,
With little desire for allegory
Transfiguring us to higher glory.
Some cheer the crucifixion of truth,
While some would fight,
Most allow reality to take flight.
Many places over-populated and underfed,
While so many escape the dread.
A world of more heat felt
As most bodies of ice melt.
Land in danger of high water.
Less flora, less fauna.
Oceans awash in flotsam and acidity
Caused by man's perfidy.
Who will awake us,
From whence will the message come?
God's crutch is abandoned,
As man's arrogance is promoted.
End times can only be avoided
If courage is exploited.

Restoration of nature
Will overcome failure.
Nothing without God's assistance
Can be accomplished.

# THE WORD

Not practiced, hardly tried
Too difficult to abide.
Words so profound and perfected
Now forlorn and neglected.
 "Love one another," an admonition
To overcome all predilection
Won't survive the expectation
As man forsakes love for hate
And like the rich man, sees Hell too late.
Two thousand years, so few witnesses
To expand the need for kindnesses.
Potential for good and change
Slips away as darkness reigns.
Wars and disputes still persist.
We have no St. Francis
To restore our sight
And to sanctify light
No one with a miracle
Or belief in transformation
As indifference is domination.
The Word is unchanged and alive
But fails to be embraced to survive.
Materialism is the focus
As we forget the least among us,
The poor, the sick, the prisoner
Too few given their chapter.

They who are the mystery of the faith
Can still give us back our grace
And cause God and the angels to applaud!

# BIEN FONDE

Out of the early New Mexico West
A dry, unpopulated, scenic territory at best.
The governor, a Civil War general,
A thinker, a lawyer, proud to be logical
Suffering loneliness and boredom
Decided to write, defending intelligent freedom.
A logical mind, proud intellect
Asserting truth to protect.
His goal, to discount religion as fanciful,
Unreliable stories, probably untruthful.
Driven by needed facts,
And a desire to cover historical tracts.
He began on page one of Genesis
Confident of showing a false thesis
One that converted so many to groundless faith
And centuries of following a questionable path.
On he read, Leviticus, Deuteronomy,
Psalms, Proverbs, Isaiah (notes flying)
Filling a mind in truth searching.
Finally Maccabees of the Old Testament
Led to St. Matthew of the New Testament.
Now comes the virgin birth,
Lending mankind a new worth?
Christ arrived full of love.
Also, full of condemnation from above.
Revolutionary ideas,
Forsaking the old

Delivering a new dramatic view:
"Forgive those who hurt you
Love thy neighbor as thyself."
"Ask me for help,
I will not give you a stone"
[Or make you feel alone].
Governor Lew Wallace read on,
Chased by the hounds of truth
Ever so reluctantly and completely,
As doubts slipped away slowly,
Did he become a convert.
And finally a convert boldly.
Out of guilt and a need for reparation
Did he decide to turn derision to exultation
A mind became faithful and pure,
He penned the story *Ben Hur.*
The cornerstone that was to be shaken,
Was transformed to a stronger foundation.

# POETRY—SPORTS

# THE GAME

When the ball is free, and in motion,
It will keep the fans' attention.
Balls, strikes, fouls, a single,
Doubles, triples, home runs mingle.
The young, the old, the rich, the poor
Come to observe the white sphere soar.
Umpires and foul lines keep honesty
In a game with little travesty.
The players are from everywhere,
Geography has little to bear.
Some have charisma and can fill the stands,
While others cannot inspire the fans.
The hope is a no-hit game,
For the pitcher to obtain the fame.
Rare is that occurrence.
Rarer still is a perfect performance.
Twenty-seven down and out magically,
But only twenty times in a century.
Enchantment, illusion, the inexplicable arises,
Perhaps leaving even God and the angels
Seeing the fun of surprises.
The game shall never die
While our Earth is bound to sky.

# DUENDE

Personal magnetism or charisma
Some have it, some do not
Ty Cobb, Calvin Coolidge, no,
Babe Ruth, Franklin Roosevelt, yes.
Why and how is just a guess;
To describe a spirit full of charm
Is not an exact or easy form.
John Kennedy, Ronald Reagan
Could impress an audience
With an extraordinary performance.
To create and exploit passion
While the listener experiences emotion,
Is a gift to be desired.
But not learned or acquired.
*Duende* enlivens our existence
Without explaining the relevance.

# POETRY—MISCELLANEOUS

# ARLINGTON BROTHERS

Two brothers in Arlington Cemetery
Warriors buried but not forgotten
These Arlington guests are only asleep
On a journey to their eternal keep
I presented my salute in remembrance
Embraced by beautiful acres of encumbrance
So many heroes at attention
All gathered at a silent convention
As much for the living as the dead
Visitors are blessed to see
Those who protected freedom's legacy
Danger lurks if obligations grow cold
And the sacrifices expended go untold
In death these heroes must live forever.

# COMIC/TRAGIC/PUNDITRY

Ranting daily with vulgar denouncements,
Ridiculing moderate pronouncements.
Down with liberals and progressives,
Up with conservative negatives.
Their own government held up to suspicion,
Taxes always in a demeaned position.
Those who do not fall in line,
Are socialist and communist of evil design.
Listeners falling for the pitch,
As hate radio and television get rich.
Double speak, flippant finger pointing,
Still listeners quickly joining.
This tyranny of meanness,
So contrived with shallowness.
Invites many to the gates of Hell,
As the willing rush there pell-mell.
They reject love of country,
Paying taxes, and honoring authority.
Let us pray that they may see
Such nearsighted inappropriate folly
Chancing a hot seat for eternity.

# LET'S PRETEND

Let's pretend they did it!
Facts, law, evidence be dammed
Emotion and noise are in command.
Repeat the lies daily
Emphasis, emphasis, lies become truth
Say it over and over again
Your opponent is full of sin
Ludicrous as it sounds, too many believe
Destroy your opposition
To obtain position
Political punditry inaccurate
Sports punditry even more incorrect
Time wasted in buffoonery
As so many fail for accuracy
Society slips away from reason
As too many swallow the poison.

# THE MAN OF THE AGES

The soul of the man!
Sorrowful, melancholy, driven, and strong,
Raised to do no wrong.
Hardly educated but a superior intellect,
Common sense was his gift to protect.
The Bible, the Declaration of Independence,
And the U.S. Constitution were his sense.
He practiced law with aplomb,
Many cases with a remarkable outcome.
He led us through a great Civil War
Proving that united we would endure.
His heart strove for those in bondage,
The perfect man for that time and age.
Socrates, Pericles, St. Francis, and Washington,
Are joined by an equal giant under the sun.

# 'A LA LUMIERE DE TROIT

Detroit, city of champions, then and now.
French founded, where the river bends.
The hub of Michigan takes a bow
This historical town making amends,
Spiritually on the rise, alive and well.
Sports and cars an excellent sell.
Cleaning up, fixing up, upward bound,
Renewed kindness for that Motown sound.
Now physically and economically upward,
No negative, no death knells forward.
All together positive motion,
Creates an excellent solution.
No need for anyone to sigh,
Because this city shall never die.

# WHAT IS LOVE

What is love?
I believe this is what love is…

As the morning sun warms the mist sending it away
Count on my love to stay

As the leaves fall in autumn and a chill fills the air
Count on my love to be there

When the sun casts shadows and you fill with doubt
Count on my love to reassure

Though nature is capricious with her wind, her rain, and her snow
Our love is sure to grow

Yes, the world is not a steady place,
Wars and trouble abound

Bur darling, you can count on my love,
As long as I am around

What is love?
I believe this is what love is…

Love can calm your heart
Lend a fresh start

Give meaning to a meaningless world

It can cause a child to smile
Making rainbows out of thunder

And love can make forever seem like a little while

Oh, it can be the answer for problems of every kind

So darling, let's put love in our mind
Yes, put love in our mind.

# MY POSSIBLE TOMBSTONE INSCRIPTIONS:

Loved and lost
Loved and won

Sympathized with the poor
Sympathized with nature

The voter got what they deserved

Believed Christ was divine, on faith and evidence.

War is a racket promoted by politicians and arms makers.

Honored my government.

Never minded taxes.

Proud moderate and fiscal conservative.

Fought to overcome foibles and sin.

Visited the prisoner.

A dreamer, not a cynic.

Tried to exercise imagination.

Fought for our children's future.

Tried to start a revolution, one with no casualties, and truth always wins.

# ACKNOWLEDGMENTS

Will Rogers used to say that all he knew he read in the newspapers. My knowledge over climate change has been taken from newspapers, Nature magazines, television, Senate hearings, email alerts, the National Weather Service and my personal observance of Michigan weather.

I have noticed that many climate change authors and scientists become timid over suggesting the possibility of end times arriving soon in the Natural world. They seem to often hold off on making dire predictions because of fear of ridicule by the deniers of climate change. I believe <u>we</u> must stand firm against the opposition. The Natural world is trending toward disaster and time is no longer a friend.

We all must advocate change. Our goal should be to leave our children a better world than the one we found. That premise should become the entire world's manifest destiny.

This book was not conceived on an island or in a vacuum. I certainly had assistance. There is abundant credit to give.

Shirley Lane, a business partner, a friend and a speedy typist has put my handwritten scribbles to type and to electronic memory. Her patience, while typing sometimes a dozen re-writes, without complaint, was a constant source of surprise to me.

My son Michael helped produce the book cover and did invaluable technical construction assistance. My son Ted kept me informed of the consequences of a lack of water in Nevada.

My friends George and Terre Voegeli, helped on a portion of reconstruction.

John Brennan, my well read racquetball partner for thirty years, was always an opinionated sounding board for my environmental positions. In addition John introduced me to a mentally different Irish leprechaun in 1976; Norman Madigan, a harmonica playing savant, who memorized every township in the State of Michigan. Norman's carbon footprint was as close to zero as anyone I ever knew. He could name every bird in Michigan. Many of us appreciated Norm as a fellow human being and took him under our wing (he died in 2010). But no one provided Norm more self worth and gave his life more meaning than John Brennan. Many of us feel the angels are waiting to applaud John someday.

I want to express my gratitude to Jim Leyland, manager of the Detroit Tiger baseball team, and to all the players. They produced a great product in 2011 that gave me a lot of respite between the rewrites that produced this book. One of my poems, The Game, arose out of a bad call by an umpire that stopped a perfect game in 2010.

I want to thank all of my family members, all of my relatives and friends who have kept life from becoming dreary by their many kindnesses.

Lastly I want to acknowledge my long deceased adoptive mother, Mertice Radtke, who saved me from an orphanage at age nine. She taught children how to read and was full of love and loyalty, throughout her life.

97690272R00054

Made in the USA
Columbia, SC
17 June 2018